PATHWAYS
BIBLE STUDY
METHOD
A better way to do Bible study...

Alan J. Lewis
Director of Pastoral Training
ReachGlobal

Cover design: JoHannah Reardon
Edited by: JoHannah Reardon and Lindsey Learn

If you would like more information about Pathways Ministries, please visit us at pathwaytrainers.com

Pathways Bible Study Method
Table of Contents

Introduction   6

The Bible Pathway   12

Careful Bible Study   18

Ask Good Questions   25

Read in Context   29

Recognize Preunderstanding   33
& Stay on the Line

Notice Linking Words   38

Write a Message Statement   42

Observe the Structure   46

Grasp the Message Flow   51

Note the Salvation Story   57

Ponder the Application   64

Review   70

Addendum   72

Leader's Questions   82

Introduction to the Pathways Bible Study Method

Rick and Shelly had been Christians for years and had attended many Bible studies, but they were weary of them all. The studies seemed to fall into three categories. Some were classes led by a teacher, often through a video. These could be interesting, but they rarely gave them opportunity to ask the hard questions. Other studies involved fill-in-the-blank questions about a given topic. These answers had become predictable, obvious, and boring to them. In the studies they liked the least, everyone just talked off the top of their head and never came to any real conclusions, leaving them more confused than when they'd begun. They were discouraged because they felt that although they read their Bibles regularly, they just didn't get much out of it. It had become duty, but it held no delight.

Jon and Laura became Christians shortly before they'd gotten married a year ago. They now attended church regularly and tried to read their Bibles, but so much of it was confusing to them. Since neither of them had read the Bible before, it was intimidating and overwhelming. They didn't even know where to begin in studying it. After reading it together during their first year of marriage, they were close to giving up on it.

Can you identify with either Rick and Shelly or Jon and Laura? Have you ever wondered why some people get so much out of the Bible when you seem to get so little? Do you struggle to hear from God as you read the Bible?

Unfortunately, many of us struggle to understand the Bible.

But be encouraged; the Pathways Bible Study is designed to make the Bible comprehensible and your study of it rich. In this study you'll learn to be a good student of the Bible, which is one of the most important things you'll ever learn because the Bible is unique and different from any other book.

The Bible is God's Word, delivered to us through the writing of human authors who were inspired by the Holy Spirit. In 2 Timothy 3:16, Paul tells us that the Scriptures are "God-breathed" (NIV); they are the product of the Spirit "breathing" the Word of God through human authors. As a result, the Bible reveals what God wants us to know about Himself and our relationship with Him, as well as His will for our lives. It's important, then, for us to accurately understand what God has said in His Word if we want to understand Him and live our lives in proper relationship to Him.

Most Christians want to live in ways that please God, and they want God to speak to them as they read the Bible. We often expect God to say something new to us to help us live for Him; but in doing so, we tend to forget that God has already spoken, telling us what He wants us to know.

It's our responsibility to discover what God has already said. We read in Hebrews 4:12 that the Word of God is "living and active," and we sometimes assume that means that God will always say something new to us. But the Bible is not living and active in the sense that it's telling us new things. It's living and active as God helps us understand what He's already said and then helps us make new applications about that to our lives.

In Hebrews 4, the author explains what the Word does in our lives—it reveals and challenges the motivations of our hearts and thoughts. So, our responsibility is threefold:

➢ Discover what God has said;
➢ Ask Him to help us understand what we've discovered;
➢ Actively apply that understanding to our lives.

It's vitally important that we make an earnest effort to

understand what He's said before we ask Him to "speak into our lives" so that we can personally apply His Word (2 Timothy 2:15)

The Pathways Bible Study Method is designed to help you make that earnest effort to understand God's Word. Over the course of the next thirteen weeks, you'll learn a step-by-step process of studying the Bible well. Each week, new tools will be added to build upon the previous sessions. You will need to come to each session, so you won't fall behind in the step-by-step process. If you have to miss a session, make sure you meet with someone in the group to catch up before rejoining the group the following week.

The method we use is fairly simple and easy to learn. We've used these principles all over the world to teach untrained pastors and lay people, both men and women, how to study the Bible. Our method is not complex and has proven to be very effective. That does not mean that Bible study will always be easy. You'll learn the tools we teach quite easily, but it will take practice, discipline, and hard work to learn how to use them well. We'll keep reminding you to depend upon the Spirit to help you, because apart from Him we'll not be able to use the tools in a way that will lead us to the insights God wants us to have.

We've designed this training to be done in a small-group Bible-study setting, because as you learn you will be able to help one another. It will also provide the accountability that we all need in order to develop new habits of study. Besides that, it's a lot more fun to work together.

This will be a working Bible study. Each member will need to put in sufficient time to study the assigned passage each week. As each new tool is added, the members will be expected to use the tool, along with the previous ones, to study the assigned passage for the next week's discussion. In the beginning this will not require a great deal of time. But as we progress, new tools and steps will be added, requiring more time to prepare. By the end of the study, you may be spending several hours preparing each week. The amount of time and effort you put into the study will determine the benefit you will receive from it and will determine how helpful you will be to the others in the group.

In this study, we ask you not to use any outside help. Please don't use study Bible notes, commentaries, or other reference materials. These all have value and benefit in study, but at this initial stage they could tempt us to take the easy route, listening to what a commentator has said rather than doing our own study. That will inhibit us from learning the tools and thinking carefully about the passages we are studying. In the future as you become more skilled, these can be helpful resources. But you should always do your own study first and then consult with commentaries and study notes to check your work.

If you are reluctant to join this study because you think it involves too much work, the following illustration may help. Imagine I ask you to help me dig up my backyard. It will be hard, backbreaking work and will take a long time. You may agree if you're my friend, but you won't be very enthusiastic. But what if I tell you that years ago a previous owner sprinkled hundreds of diamonds in the backyard and you may keep every diamond you find? How would that knowledge change your attitude about the work? That's the way it is with careful Bible study. You must work at it, but the rewards are enormous, more valuable than diamonds.

The Importance of Prayer
The Pathways Bible Study Method is designed to teach you the fundamental tools of Bible study so that you can understand what God has said and be well prepared to receive the Spirit's application of His Word to your life. All of God's people have the capacity to read, study, and understand what He's said. Learning to study well will enhance your ability to feed yourself from the Word in your Bible study, reading, and devotions. We hope it will also equip many to teach God's people directly from His Word rather than always using someone else's study material. Ask

His help as you seek to grow and to help others grow through His Word.

How to Use This Bible Study Guide

Plan on completing one session each time you meet. The first meeting will provide an introduction and starting point for the study.

This method can be used with any passage of Scripture, but we recommend that you start with a study of a short New Testament epistle. We'll use the book of 1 Thessalonians as our example throughout this study. That will allow you and your group to use the full range of basic tools to study an entire book.

In the initial meeting to go over this introduction, make sure each person has this study guide and explain what will be expected of each participant. At that time, explain the first week's task, which is to read the book of 1 Thessalonians through several times during the week and to read through "Session #1: The Bible Pathway."

Each week following the introduction, you will learn a new tool, which you will immediately put into practice. A few specialized tools will be added in an addendum that can be used with different types of literature in the Bible, such as poetry or parables. Allow ninety minutes for your meeting and structure the study as follows:

> ➤ Come prepared. Be sure you've read that week's session and have done the assignment ahead of time.
> ➤ Start with a brief social time—and start on time.
> ➤ Ask God the Holy Spirit to help you as you discuss His Word.
> ➤ Using the Leader's Questions at the end of this book, plan on a discussion that lasts approximately one hour. During that hour, make sure everyone understands the "Defining Terms" indicated in each session of that week's lesson. Ask them to jot down any questions they may have. Then discuss what everyone has learned

from the passage of the week, using the tools you've put into practice from the last step.

➤ Provide a short time at the end of the discussion for thoughtful application of what you've learned and remind everyone to do the next session on their own in preparation for the following week's study.

➤ Be sure to close in prayer, thanking God for His help and blessing in the study.

As you get started, the discussion may not flow easily, but as you get used to the method and each other, it will get better and better. We're excited about introducing you to this Bible study. Many who have used this study have greatly benefitted, especially those who have used it to teach others how to study. We hope it's a blessing to you as well.

Session #1

The Bible Pathway

PURPOSE OF THIS SESSION: To help you understand what it means to find and stay on what we call "The Bible Pathway."

FORMAT: Although this is the first session, each person should have read this session, "The Bible Pathway," ahead of time and completed the assignment before coming. In your time together, ask if anyone has any questions about "The Bible Pathway." As a group, help each other answer those questions. When each person feels he or she understands the concept, discuss what everyone learned through the assignment, including any questions they may have. When finished, assign Session #2 for next week.

We're all familiar with what it means to travel on a path. We walk on sidewalks to get from house to house, hike a trail to get through the woods, and, for the more adventurous among us, trek cross country. Even in a city, we use paths in parks and through gardens.

Walking on a path not only is a means of travel but can also be a means of learning. We learn about the people and places we meet along the way; about the plants and animals we encounter and the scenery we see. Walking down a familiar path is one way of connecting with our community and experiencing life. Walking a new path often allows us to expand our lives and experience new things.

Studying the Bible can be viewed in much the same way as walking on a path. As we read through the Bible, we learn new things. The more often we read the same passages, the more familiar we become with what we find there. The things we discover as we read enrich our lives and help us connect with God and with others around us. When we read new sections of the Bible, we encounter new ideas that expand our thinking and our lives.

Learning to walk on a new path requires some patience and direction from those who've been there before. Learning to study the Bible is like that as well. There are new skills to learn and habits to develop if we are going to do a good job walking through the Bible's teachings.

This course is designed to take you down the path of how to study and teach the Bible. Once you've mastered these skills, you'll be able to walk down all the pathways of the Bible and gain great understanding about what God has said in His Word, and you will be able to share that understanding effectively with others. We hope this will be a fun, challenging, and fruitful adventure for you. Our hope is that you will be blessed and that God's kingdom will be advanced.

Defining Terms: What is the "The Bible Pathway"?

When we hurry along a pathway, we want the shortest, straightest path to our destination. But we often find that impossible because something blocks the path—perhaps a river or a mountain. Sometimes a danger along the way makes the shortest path unwise. So, we have to take a path that curves and takes longer to travel if we're going to arrive safely at our destination. This principle is also true of our path to understanding the Bible.

We're often in a hurry to understand what God has to say to us in His Word. We want to apply the Bible to our lives immediately. But there are at least two major problems blocking our way:

1) The Bible was not written directly to us but to people who lived a long time ago in cultures sometimes far different from ours. The Bible was not written *to* us, but it was written *for* us. If we do not take time to first understand what the author was saying to the original readers, we're in danger of misunderstanding God's message to us.

2) We are sometimes tempted to approach the Bible from our own cultural and personal outlook, often reading into the passage what is not there. Once again, we need to try to understand what was in the author's mind as he wrote to a specific person or set of people in a specific historical setting. Once we understand that, we can then ask, "What is God saying to us in our time and culture?" The following diagram illustrates this process, which we call "The Bible Pathway."

The Bible Pathway

Sometimes this path to the original readers is quite obvious and at other times it's not. For example, the Bible gives specific instructions in Exodus about how to sacrifice bulls. Do you follow these instructions when you sacrifice bulls in your church? Of course not, because we realize we no longer have to sacrifice animals. Why not? Because God is not commanding *us* to sacrifice animals, even though He did expect the original readers to do so.

We live in a different time and under a different covenant from that of the people of the Old Testament (Hebrews 8:13). We're no longer under the law. We live under the new covenant as a result of Christ's final sacrifice for us. So, although we can't apply all that's said in the Old Testament directly to our lives, we can apply the spiritual principles found there. While we should not start sacrificing animals, we can learn about the principles of sacrifice, and that will help us learn about Christ's sacrifice for us.

At other times the difference between the original readers and us is much more difficult to see, especially in the New Testament. But if we are going to hear God's message to us, we first need to hear His message given through the author to the original readers. We must *observe* and *understand* what the author said in the original time and setting, and then we can think about how to apply his message in our time and setting.

As we learn to study the Bible carefully, we'll always travel on this "Bible Pathway" of understanding what God was saying first to the original readers and then how He intends that to apply to us. Through this course we will gradually add steps and tools along the "Bible Pathway" to help you study well.

You'll want to work through each step in every passage that you study. You'll also use the tools as needed in your study depending on what passage you're working on. The purpose of this course is not to tell you what the Bible says, but to help *you* discover what the Bible says. If you follow these steps and use these tools, you'll discover the Bible's meaning. The following is the completed "Bible Pathway" we will use for this course:

Bible Pathway

God's Message

No

Prayer

Us

Original Reader

1. Observation: Ask Good Questions
2. Context
3. Structure/Flow/Message Statement
4. The Bible's Salvation Story

6. Application   5. Present-day Statement

**Assignment: Read 1 Thessalonians and study
1 Thessalonians 1**

Read the entire book of 1 Thessalonians on your own this week and answer the following questions:

- From what you read, what conclusions can you come to about who the original readers were?
- Is this church or person mentioned in the book of Acts or elsewhere in the Bible? (A word search using a tool such as biblegateway.com will help you determine this.)
- From your reading, can you guess why this book was written to the original readers?

Carefully read 1 Thessalonians 1.

➤ In a sentence or two, state what you think the author of the book intended to say to his original readers in this chapter.
➤ How do you think he wanted them to apply this message to their lives? Do you think the application to your life might be slightly different? How?

Application: It's very important that we not only study the Word of God well, but that we respond to what we've learned. Is there anything that the Spirit has impressed you with this week from your study of 1 Thessalonians 1 that you can apply to your life (an application can be what we do, how we think, or what we love)?

Note: We will spend the first three sessions on 1 Thessalonians 1. This may seem tedious, but it will help you learn how to study a passage carefully.

Here is an example from Philippians 3:1–11 showing how an answer to this assignment might look:

Finally, my brothers, rejoice in the Lord. To write the same things to you is no trouble to me and is safe for you

Look out for the dogs, look out for the evildoers, look out for those who mutilate the flesh. For we are the real circumcision, who worship by the Spirit of God and glory in Christ Jesus and put no confidence in the flesh—though I myself have reason for confidence in the flesh also. If anyone else thinks he has reason for confidence in the flesh, I have more: circumcised on the eighth day, of the people of Israel, of the tribe of Benjamin, a Hebrew of Hebrews; as to the law, a Pharisee; as to zeal, a persecutor of the church; as to righteousness, under the law blameless. But whatever gain I had, I counted as a loss for the sake of Christ. Indeed, I count everything as loss because of the surpassing worth of knowing Christ Jesus my Lord. For his sake I have suffered the loss of all things and count them as rubbish, in order that I may gain Christ and be found in him, not having a righteousness of my own that comes from the law, but that which comes through faith in Christ, the righteousness from God that depends on faith—that I may know him and the power of his resurrection, and may share his sufferings, becoming like him in his death, that by any means possible I may attain the resurrection from the dead.

Answer: I think Paul wanted them to understand that his Jewish religious achievements counted for nothing in God's eyes. I don't have Jewish religious achievements, but I have Christian ones that I cannot take pride or credit in.

Session #2
Careful Bible Study

PURPOSE OF THIS SESSION: To explain what it means to do "Careful Bible Study" by discussing the different steps involved and practicing together.

FORMAT: Each person should have read this "Careful Bible Study" session ahead of time and completed the assignment before coming. In your time together, ask if anyone has any questions about this session. As a group, help each other answer those questions. When each person feels he or she understands the concept, discuss what everyone learned through the assignment, including any questions they may have. When finished, assign Session #3 for next week.

In the last session we talked about "The Bible Pathway." We emphasized the need to discover what the author intended to say to the original readers before we ask what God intends us to learn from the passage. As we go on in this study, we'll be adding more steps and tools to help us in this.

Remember that our first step in studying the Bible is prayer. Don't forget to take time to seriously ask God to help you understand His Word. Once you have an attitude of dependence and trust in Him, you're ready for the second step. We call this step "Careful Bible Study."

Defining Terms: What is "Careful Bible Study"?
"Careful Bible study" is what some people call "inductive Bible study." We don't use the term *inductive* because it's sometimes hard for people to understand that word, especially in foreign cultures. "Careful Bible Study" contains three steps: *Observation, Understanding,* and *Application.*

Because we believe that the Bible is the Word of God and communicates God's thoughts to us, we want to respect His

Word by being careful to accurately understand what it says. We don't want to impose our ideas onto the Bible but rather listen closely to what God is saying to us through His Word. That simply means that we must carefully read what is written, paying close attention to what is actually said. As we examine the text, we then gradually come to a conclusion about what the author of the passage intended to say. Once we understand what he intended to say, we then can consider how to apply that message to our lives.

We want to be careful to keep these three steps in proper order. If we try to apply before we understand, we may miss God's intent for our lives. If we try to understand before we observe, we may misunderstand God's message. Throughout this process, we depend upon God's Spirit to help us *see* what is said, to *understand* it correctly, and to *apply* it wisely to our lives. That's why our study process always must begin with prayer. We need God's help to understand and apply His Word. Let's look at these three parts of "Careful Bible Study."

Step#1: Reading and Observation After praying, we must begin our study by reading, and not just casually reading, but carefully reading the passage. It's important to read the passage several times, paying close attention to observe what is said. Sometimes it may be helpful to read the passage out loud or even to copy the passage onto a piece of paper. This can help us slow down and notice everything that's written in the passage. As we read, we should focus on determining what the author said to the original readers:

- What are obvious things we can see from the text?
- Are there any commands in the passage?
- What words are repeated throughout the passage?
- Is there something written that surprises you or seems of special interest?
- Is the author comparing two different things in the passage?

We want to take time to carefully read and study what the author has written. As we grow in our ability to observe, we'll develop the ability to see the author's "flow of thought" (sequence of ideas). We want to notice how he develops his ideas.

It's helpful to remember that observations cannot be disagreed with. We are simply stating what's there. If someone can disagree with us, we've moved from observing to understanding the meaning of the passage. We should observe the passage carefully before we decide what the passage means.

Examples of observation from Romans 12:3–5:

1. What Paul says is based on the grace given to him.
2. It applies to all in the church.
3. We're not to think more highly of ourselves than we ought to.
4. We're to think with God's judgment.
5. That is according to how God has allotted to each a measure of faith.
6. We're like a body with many members but different functions.
7. We are many, but one body, and members of one another.

Step#2: Understanding
Once we have carefully observed what's written, we need to try to understand what the passage means. We're trying to understand what the original author was thinking when he wrote the passage. We want to understand what he intended to say and what his purpose was for writing. In order to do that, we must first understand the meaning of the words that he uses.

We may have to look up the definitions of words we don't understand. Then we can consider the significance of the words that are used. An important step will be to decide on the major points in the passage.

Taking into consideration the things we've observed, we need to prayerfully think or meditate on what we've read. This takes time and effort but bears fruit in understanding. As we reflect on the passage, we need to consider how the message of this passage fits in with what we've learned elsewhere in the book we are studying or in the Bible as a whole.

An important part of reflection is to ask how the passage relates to the gospel and God's grace in my life. As we seek understanding, it's sometimes helpful to summarize what the passage says in our own words. As our understanding grows, we should be able to restate the main thing the author intended to say in a single sentence.

Step#3: Application

After we've read and examined the passage and come to a conclusion about what the author intended to say, we're ready to consider how to apply that message to our lives. We should notice if the passage offers an application in the text itself. Our applications should address what we do, how we think, and what we love.

There may be new truths to believe or changes that we need to make in our thinking or in the way that we live. We may simply be encouraged by new insights into God's goodness or promises. We may need to take specific actions of obedience or to repent of specific sins or attitudes.

In all of this, we need always to respond directly to God Himself in prayer, praise, commitment, obedience, or fellowship. God communicates with us in His Word and wants to draw us into a closer relationship with Himself. In all our applications we should remember that through Jesus we have complete forgiveness of sins (past, present, and future), and that we are fully and deeply loved by God. As we apply the Word to our lives, it should always draw us to Christ, for apart from Him we can do nothing. If we want to grow and change, we need to do so in union with Him.

Using our Bible Pathway diagram, we can show how observation, understanding, and application help us get the message God has for us.

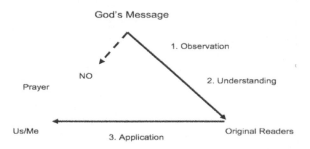

These three steps are the beginning of our journey to understanding the passage. As we learn how to complete these steps well, we'll add other steps and tools along the pathway to help us better understand each passage we study. Every tool we introduce in this study will help us observe better, understand more fully, or apply the Word to our lives more effectively.

Assignment: Make Observations from 1 Thessalonians 1
In this assignment we will concentrate on observation. Both observation and prayer are foundational in our study of God's Word. Everything else we do in Bible study will be dependent upon the quality of our observations. So, we want to work hard at learning how to be good observers of the text.

Carefully re-read 1 Thessalonians 1. As you read, observe thoroughly what you see. Write down as many observations as you can about the passage. Some of these observations may be words: important words, repeated words, surprising words, or difficult words you may not understand.

Some of your observations may be about ideas. Again, these ideas may be important, repeated, surprising, or hard to understand. You may also want to notice the sequence of ideas, or how they are connected. Write down anything else about the passage that you think is important or interesting. Be prepared to share your observations in your next group session.

If possible, try to do this assignment over several different days. Each day may bring a new perspective and you may observe more. After several days of observing, spend some time pondering what you think the author intended to say to the original readers: Why does he begin the way he does? What are his main points?

Application: Finally, think about how this might apply to your own life, asking God to help you understand how He wants you to respond to the passage. Often as we study the Word, God uses it to show us how our lives are in some way out of line with Him. Is there anything you've read or studied this week that made you realize that your life is not fully in harmony with God, His character, and His thoughts? In what ways might you be encouraged by God's Spirit to make a change in your life?

Here is an example from Philippians 3:1–7
showing how to do this kind of observation:

Finally, my brothers, rejoice in the Lord. To write the same things to you is no trouble to me and is safe for you
   Look out for the dogs, look out for the evildoers, look out for those who mutilate the flesh. For we are the real circumcision, who worship by the Spirit of God and glory in Christ Jesus and put no confidence in the flesh—though I myself have reason for confidence in the flesh also. If anyone else thinks he has reason for confidence in the flesh, I have more: circumcised on the eighth day, of the people of Israel, of the tribe of Benjamin, a Hebrew of Hebrews; as to the law, a Pharisee; as to zeal, a persecutor of the church; as to righteousness, under the law blameless. But whatever gain I had, I counted as a loss for the sake of Christ.

- Rejoice in the Lord
- Paul has no trouble writing about these things and feels it's safe for them.
- Paul warns them to look out for evildoers (he calls them dogs!)—those who mutilate the flesh.
- We are the circumcision, who worship by the Spirit of God and glory in Christ Jesus.
- We put no confidence in the flesh.
- Then Paul lists all the reasons he would have for confidence in the flesh: circumcised on the eighth day, of the people of Israel, of the tribe of Benjamin, a Hebrew of Hebrews; as to the law, a Pharisee; as to zeal, a persecutor of the church; as to righteousness under the law, blameless.
- But whatever gain Paul had, he counted it as loss for the sake of Christ.

Session #3
Ask Good Questions

PURPOSE OF THIS SESSION: To learn to ask good
questions of the text so that we can begin to understand
what it means.

FORMAT: Each person should have read this "Ask Good
Questions" session ahead of time and completed the
assignment before coming. In your time together, ask if
anyone has any questions about this session. As a group,
help each other answer those questions. When each person
feels he or she understands the concept, discuss what
everyone learned through the assignment, including any
questions they may have. When finished, assign Session #4
for next week.

After prayer, observation is a foundational step in Careful
Bible Study. Everything else we do in Bible study depends on
these two things. But our goal is to come to a good
understanding of the passage—first understanding what the
author intended to say as he wrote to the original readers, and
then understanding God's intent for us. This week we
introduce a tool called "Ask Good Questions" that helps us
bridge the gap between observation and understanding.

Defining Terms: What are good questions?
Asking good questions helps us observe more carefully what's
written in the Bible, which allows us to understand it better.
This is a great skill that helps us focus our attention on what
the author of the text meant to say. Asking good questions
helps us move beyond reading the Bible casually to carefully
observing and understanding what it's saying. Asking

questions helps us discover insights that we otherwise might not see. When we try to find answers to our questions, we often discover how much we don't know about a passage and what we need to study further. What are good questions? They are questions that help us understand the author's intent. See the following examples:

- ➤ **Who** are the people involved in the passage? Who is speaking? Who is listening?
- ➤ **What** is happening? What is being said? What is surprising about this? What are the key words in the passage? What is the tone of the passage? What are the connections between this passage and other verses around it?
- ➤ **When** did this happen? What is the sequence of events or thoughts?
- ➤ **Where** did it take place? What places are mentioned?
- ➤ **Why** did the author say this? What's his purpose? Is it stated? Why does he say it here?
- ➤ **How** did it happen? How does the author describe what happened? How would the original readers have heard this message?

We can also ask questions about the meaning of certain words or about the significance of the words the author has chosen to use. In summary, what would you ask the author if he were here to explain what he said?

Because God is ultimately the Author of the Bible, we can ask Him to help us understand. We should also ask Him for discernment about the kinds of questions that we ask and for perseverance in our study until we fully understand His message.

Assignment: Ask Good Questions of 1 Thessalonians 1
Prepare a sheet of paper with two columns, one for observations and one for questions.

Observations	Questions

Once again study 1 Thessalonians 1, filling in the columns with your observations on each verse and any questions you have related to those observations. You can also jot down any conclusions you've come to from those questions.

Taking time to write them down will help you focus on and remember key points you've thought about as you've studied. If you don't write down your observations and questions, you may forget them in the course of your study.

Application: Another way the Bible may confront us with a need for change is in the way that we act or live. Are you aware of any way that the Lord is prompting you to change your actions as a result of your study?

Here is an example from Philippians 3:2-3:

Look out for the dogs, look out for the evildoers, look out for those who mutilate the flesh. For we are the real circumcision, who worship by the Spirit of God and glory in Christ Jesus and put no confidence in the flesh...

Observations: Paul warns them to look out for evildoers (dogs) who mutilate the flesh. We who worship by God's Spirit and glory in Christ are the circumcision. We put no confidence in the flesh.

Questions: Who are the evildoers? Why does he call them dogs? How do they mutilate flesh? Who is "we"? What does it mean to worship by God's Spirit and to glory in Christ? Is circumcision the mutilation from verse 2? Why does Paul put no confidence in the flesh?

Session #4

Read in Context

PURPOSE OF THIS SESSION: To explain what it means to read a passage in context and to practice doing it together.

FORMAT: Each person should have read this "Read In Context" session ahead of time and completed the assignment before coming. In your time together, ask if anyone has any questions about this session. As a group, help each other answer those questions. When each person feels he or she understands the concept, discuss what everyone learned through the assignment, including any questions they may have. When finished, assign Session #5 for next week.

As we travel on The Bible Pathway to understanding the Bible, we need to understand the concept of the context, or the surroundings, of the passage we are going to study. The context for any passage we study is made up of the verses that surround it. The idea of context is much like the idea of community.

We all live in communities. We have relationships with many people who live around us, and these relationships give meaning to our lives and influence us greatly. Some of these relationships are close and some are more distant. The people we are closest to influence our lives the most. Those who are more distant influence us less.

The same is true of words and ideas in the Bible. None of the words in the Bible exist alone. All are found in relation to other words found in the Bible. The words and ideas in any passage we study are surrounded by many other words and ideas—those found in the passages that precede and follow the passage we are studying. These surrounding words and ideas have an impact on what the words we are studying mean.

Defining Terms: What is context?
The words that we find closest to the ones we are studying (for example, the verse that precedes the one we are studying) have the most impact on what the verse we are studying means. Words found farther away, perhaps in previous or later paragraphs, chapters, or books, have less influence on what the words in our verse mean. If we want to understand what any verse, paragraph, or chapter of the Bible means, we must consider what the verses, paragraphs, and chapters around them mean. These words form the context of the verses we are studying. This is one of the most important tools for accurately understanding the Bible.

In order to understand the context of a passage, we must read the passages surrounding it. Once again, we must observe what the author says in these passages and try to understand what he intended to say. As we study our way through a book, it's important to remember what we learned in the previous passages, because those passages will influence the meaning of what we are reading now. If we studied the last passage well, it will help us understand the present passage better.

But it's also important to consider what lies ahead. Where the ideas in the book are going also influences our understanding of the meaning of the passage. We may not know the meaning of future passages, as well as previous ones, but having a general understanding of what is coming later will help us see the author's purpose. That is one of the reasons why it's important to read the whole book through several times before beginning to study passage by passage.

As we consider the context, we will be looking at the connections between the passages we study. If we consider the major ideas of each passage we study, we can better see how they connect with each other. As we make these connections, we'll begin to see the path of understanding the author is taking us on as we travel through the book. When we finish, we'll better understand the author's purpose in writing the book and the major ideas he wanted us to learn.

Practice Together. (There is no need to do this on your own. We will cover this when we meet as a group.)

Form groups of three. Before you open your Bibles, write out what you think the following verses mean:

Philippians 4:13 "I can do all things through Him who strengthens me."

Revelation 3:20 "Here I am! I stand at the door and knock. If anyone hears my voice and opens the door, I will come in and eat with that person, and they with me." (NIV)

Matthew 6:33 "But seek first the kingdom of God and His righteousness, and all these things will be added to you."

Now, in your groups, go back and read the context of these verses and answer the following question: After reading some of the surrounding verses, how does your understanding of each of these verses change?

> ➤ Philippians 4:10–16
> ➤ Revelation 3:14–22
> ➤ Matthew 6:24–34

Each group of three: share with the larger group some of the most important changes in understanding that you gained as a group by looking at these individual verses in context.

Assignment: Study 1 Thessalonians 2:1–12 in context
This week we'll study 1 Thessalonians 2:1–12. Don't forget to

fill in the two columns of observations and questions as you study. As you do that, think about what you've learned in 1 Thessalonians 1. How might that influence your understanding as you come to this chapter? As you read chapter 2, you might want to look ahead at chapter 3 so that you understand the context of chapter 2.

Application: When you apply this passage, consider that the Bible convicts us to change the way we *think*. Is there anything you've learned this week that points out how your thinking needs to change? How can you grow to think more like Christ?

For an example of context, look to Philippians 3:2–3:

Look out for the dogs, look out for the evildoers, look out for those who mutilate the flesh. For we are the real circumcision, who worship by the Spirit of God and glory in Christ Jesus and put no confidence in the flesh...

Philippians 3:2 leaves us wondering what Paul is talking about. Who are the evildoers? Why are they mutilating flesh? But if we read verse 3, we understand that the evildoers are those who insist that Christians be circumcised, and that's the mutilation Paul is talking

---

Session #5

Recognize Preunderstanding
& Stay on the Line

PURPOSE OF THIS SESSION: To explain how our previous understanding of a passage colors the way we read it, and how important it is not to say more or less than what Scripture says.

FORMAT: Each person should have read this "Recognize Preunderstanding & Stay on the Line" session ahead of time and completed the assignment before coming. In your time together, ask if anyone has any questions about this session. As a group, help each other answer those questions. When each person feels he or she understands the concept, discuss what everyone learned through the assignment, including any questions they may have. When finished, assign Session #6 for next week.

This week we will focus on some principles that we need to keep in mind as we study the Bible. These are not exactly study tools but are important principles to follow. The first of these we call "preunderstanding."

Defining Terms: What is preunderstanding?
Preunderstanding describes all the ideas and perspectives that we bring to the text *before* we begin to study it. Some have called this term "presuppositions." We've been taught many things about the Bible, have thought about what we believe,

and may have even studied the passage before and come to some conclusions about what it means. Some passages are very familiar to us because we've read them many times and assume we know what they teach. And sometimes we decide what we want to believe and look for a passage that supports that idea.

We're often less aware of other aspects of our understanding — things, for instance, that we've learned from our families, our culture, and our experiences. At times we may be unaware of how strongly our theological convictions govern how we look at a text. We may not see what the passage is really saying because it doesn't fit neatly with our theological understanding, especially if that understanding is commonly held and assumed by everyone in our church. We bring all of these ideas and understandings, both consciously and unconsciously, to the text before we begin to study.

Some aspects of preunderstanding are helpful and necessary. What we know and understand helps us learn new things and put them into perspective. Other aspects are not so positive. We often fill gaps in the text with our cultural or biblical understanding, and that can lead us to misunderstand what the author intended to say. Also, our preunderstanding can limit the possibilities of what the text says. We think, *It can't mean that because I've been taught something else.*

None of us approaches the study of Scripture from a neutral point of view without any preunderstanding, and we don't want to ignore everything we already know before we begin our study. We want to build on all that God has taught us in the past from His Word when we come to our present study. But if we're going to do "Careful Bible Study" there are several things we need to keep in mind about our preunderstanding.

1. Our current understanding is always partial and imperfect. Even the apostle Paul admitted that. In 1 Corinthians 13:12 he says, "For now we see in a mirror dimly, but then face to face. Now I know in part; but then I shall know fully, even as I have been fully known."

2. Although our understanding is always imperfect, the Bible is perfect. It is God's Word, "breathed out" by Him through the various authors of Scripture (2 Timothy 3:16). Therefore we must submit our present understanding to the text. We must always be ready to adjust what we think and believe according to what the text actually says. Sometimes that may mean only a slight adjustment to our thinking or a deepening of our understanding. At other times we may need to radically change what we think or believe. We must always be open to having our cultural or theological thinking challenged and adjusted by Scripture.

3. We are not trying to come to the text with a completely blank understanding, which is impossible. That's not our goal. We're coming to the text with a submissive attitude, asking God to teach us from His Word.

Steps to Deal with Preunderstanding:
1. Come to the text with a *submissive* attitude. The text must shape our understanding. We must never adjust the meaning of the text to fit our understanding.

2. Come to the text with a *dependent* attitude. We depend upon the Holy Spirit to guide and teach us as we study. We're not to study the Word independently of Him. We should ask Him to continually adjust our understanding to match His Word (Ephesians 4:15).

3. Come to the text with a *disciplined* attitude. We must study carefully and work with the Holy Spirit if we are going to understand what the text actually says.

Defining Terms: What does it mean to stay on the line?
Dick Lucas, a Church of England pastor who has taught many to study the Scriptures well, first coined the term "Staying on

the Line." As we study, we come to conclusions about what God has said in His Word. But we must be careful to say no more than what the passage says, and no less. This principle is illustrated by a simple line, which represents what God's Word actually says:

No!

_____Yes!_____God's Word

No!

Don't Go Above the Line
To go above the line means that we add something to what God has said in His Word. It means to say more than God has said or to say something different from what He has said. Most of us are guilty of occasionally adding things to what the text of Scripture says. We do that when we assume certain things are true. Perhaps it's something we've always believed or have been taught. It might actually be true, but the passage we are studying doesn't say it. To add to what God has said is a serious error. We're substituting our words for His.

Don't Go Below the Line
We can also go below the line and say less than what the Bible says. We do this by skipping, ignoring, or explaining away things we read that we do not like or understand. Sometimes our culture blinds us to what the Bible says and causes us to miss some of its teaching. At other times we may not study as hard as we should and so we miss some important things that a passage is teaching. At times we need to confess that we aren't positive what the author meant by something he wrote. We need to be patient as God teaches us, but we should always *attempt* to understand everything in a passage. If we can't fully understand at the present time, we know that's something we need to work on in the future.

Assignment: Study 1 Thessalonians 2:13–20

Walk through the study steps for 1 Thessalonians 2:13–20. As you study this week, ask God to help you keep in mind your preunderstanding and to help you use it wisely. Ask Him to help you be submissive to His Word, dependent on His help, and disciplined in your study. Check yourself to make sure you stay on the line.

Application: As you consider application, is there anything you've encountered this week in your study that may indicate a need to change or refine your beliefs?

> To see an example of preunderstanding, look at this example from Philippians 3:7:
>
> But whatever gain I had, I counted as a loss for the sake of Christ.
>
> In the past I thought of that "gain" as material things. But that's not what Paul is talking about in this context. Although it can be applied that way, that's not what the passage is about.

Session #6

Notice Linking Words

PURPOSE OF THIS SESSION: To explain that linking words show us how different parts of a passage relate to each other.

FORMAT: Each person should have read this "Notice Linking Words" session ahead of time and completed the assignment. In your time together, answer any questions anyone has about this concept. When each person feels he or she understands the concept, discuss what everyone learned through the assignment, including any questions they may have. When finished, assign Session #7 for next week.

Linking words in the Bible connect ideas as signs often connect roads. Road signs tell us which way to go to get to our destination. They help us understand how the road we are on is connected with roads we encounter along the way. Linking words help us understand how the different parts of a passage relate to each other and help us find the meaning of the Bible passage we are studying. They also remind us to look at what comes before and what will come after.

Defining Terms: What are linking words?

Linking words connect one idea in the passage with other ideas, much as links in a chain connect one part to the other. They show us the *reason for* or the *result of* what is said. We can think of them as arrows pointing the way. The chart on the next page gives you examples of common English linking words and what they mean. This is not a comprehensive chart, but it will give you a good idea of what we are talking about.

Examples of linking words:

Word	Meaning
Therefore	Logical conclusion
And	Connects two thoughts
But	Contrasts two thoughts
Consequently	Gives a conclusion
For this reason	Gives a reason (obviously ☺)
Thus	Gives a conclusion
So	Gives a reason, result, purpose, or next step
Because	Gives an explanation of what came before
Since	Gives a reason or explanation of a main idea
For	Gives a reason or explanation of a main idea
So that	Tells purpose or result of something

Working with Linking Words

If we are going to stay on the path to understanding what a passage in the Bible means, we have to pay special attention to the linking words. When we see these words, we should ask: How do the linking words connect ideas in this passage? How do they help with the development of thought in this passage?

Examples of linking words from 1 Thessalonians:

(These may vary according to the translation of the Bible you are using, but even if they do, they will tell you something about how that verse is connected to the one before it.)

1:5: "for" (or "because") — Paul explains how he knows that God had chosen the Thessalonians.

1:7: "so that" — Paul says the Thessalonians became imitators of him and the Lord *with the result that* they became an example to others.

Look at the sequence of the word "for" or "because" in 1:8–9; 2:1, 3, 5, 9, 14, 18–20. In each case a reason precedes it. In the midst of this sequence we have another linking word, "but" (showing contrast), in 2:4, 7, 17.

Assignment: Study 1 Thessalonians 3:1–5
Go through the steps of study, observation, questions, and context. Remember to ask God's help with each step. Then look for linking words. Write down the ones you find and explain the role they play in the passage.

Application: In the last two sessions we considered how the passage could be applied to our lives in how we think, act, or live. Another way we may consider how to apply the Word is in what we *love*. Do you notice anything from this passage that causes you to ask God to redirect the affections of your heart to match His?

Look at this example of identifying linking words from Philippians 3:2–4:

Look out for the dogs, look out for the evildoers, look out for those who mutilate the flesh. For we are the real circumcision, who worship by the Spirit of God and glory in Christ Jesus and put no confidence in the flesh—though I myself have reason for confidence in the flesh also.

Verse 3: "For" directs us back to verse 2 and helps explain the meaning of that verse.

Verse 4: "though" forces us to look back at verse 3 to see that this "confidence in the flesh" is not a good thing.

Write a Message Statement

PURPOSE OF THIS SESSION: To state the overall message of the passage in one sentence.

FORMAT: Each person should have read "Write a Message Statement" ahead of time and completed the assignment before coming. In your time together, ask if anyone has any questions about this session. As a group, help each other answer those questions. When each person feels he or she understands the concept, discuss what everyone learned through the assignment, including any questions they may have. When finished, assign Session #8 for next week.

When we are trying to understand the meaning of a passage, it's helpful to state the message of the passage in a single sentence. This sentence is called the "message statement." * We try to determine what the author's main points are and then try to organize those points into a sentence that states the author's purpose.

Defining Terms: Message Statement
The message statement is the focal point around which the other ideas in the passage are organized. Doing the hard work of trying to write the author's purpose in a single sentence helps us think clearly about the passage.

We should first write a sentence that describes the author's message to the original reader or readers. We call this our "Original Message Statement." Later we can write one that describes God's message to us. The Message Statement answers two central questions:

1. What is this passage talking about? This is the subject of the passage and could be one word or a short phrase.
2. What is it saying about the subject? These are the things that the passage says about the subject.

We want to answer these two questions and then try to write a single, complete sentence that not only states the subject but also captures what the passage says about it. This sentence should be relatively short, twelve to sixteen words.

Example 1: 1 Timothy 5:1–2
"Do not rebuke an older man but encourage him as you would a father. Treat younger men like brothers, older women like mothers, younger women like sisters, in all purity."

What is the subject of this passage? We have to think, *What is the author's main point here?* The subject or main point might be stated: How believers should treat each other.

What does it say about that? It says:
- ➢ Treat older men as you would treat your father.
- ➢ Treat younger men as a brother.
- ➢ Treat older women as you would treat your mother.
- ➢ Treat younger women with respect as you would treat your sisters.

Putting the subject and what it says about that subject together in one sentence, we might say: "In the church we should treat one another as family members."

Example 2: James 1:2–8
"Count it all joy, my brothers, when you meet trials of various kinds, for you know that the testing of your faith produces steadfastness. And let steadfastness have its full effect, that you may be perfect and complete, lacking in nothing.

"If any of you lacks wisdom, let him ask God, who gives generously to all without reproach, and it will be given him. But let him ask in faith, with no doubting, for the one who doubts is like a wave of the sea that is driven and tossed by the wind. For that person must not suppose that he will receive anything from the Lord; he is a double-minded man, unstable in all his ways."

What is the subject of this passage?
It could be stated: How to be complete.

What does the passage say about that?
  - ➤ When we joyfully endure trials, we are made complete.
  - ➤ If we lack wisdom, we can ask God in faith and He will give it to us.

Our message statement might then be: We become complete by joyfully enduring trials and asking God in faith for wisdom.

Assignment: Study 1 Thessalonians 3:6–13
Follow the other steps we have covered so far in this study and write a message statement for this passage.

Application: As you think about application, what is the most significant thing God has impressed on you in these passages? Spend some time this week talking to God about what that would look like in your life.

*Many of the concepts covered in this section are based on Haddon Robinson's *Biblical Preaching* (Baker Academic, 1981) pp. 31-48.

Here is an example of a message statement based on Philippians 3:2–11:

Look out for the dogs, look out for the evildoers, look out for those who mutilate the flesh. For we are the real circumcision, who worship by the Spirit of God and glory in Christ Jesus and put no confidence in the flesh—though I myself have reason for confidence in the flesh also. If anyone else thinks he has reason for confidence in the flesh, I have more: circumcised on the eighth day, of the people of Israel, of the tribe of Benjamin, a Hebrew of Hebrews; as to the law, a Pharisee; as to zeal, a persecutor of the church; as to righteousness, under the law blameless. But whatever gain I had, I counted as a loss for the sake of Christ. Indeed, I count everything as loss because of the surpassing worth of knowing Christ Jesus my Lord. For his sake I have suffered the loss of all things and count them as rubbish, in order that I may gain Christ and be found in him, not having a righteousness of my own that comes from the law, but that which comes through faith in Christ, the righteousness from God that depends on faith—that I may know him and the power of his resurrection, and may share his sufferings, becoming like him in his death, that by any means possible I may attain the resurrection from the dead.

Message Statement: Do not fall into thinking you have to earn your standing with God, but realize that our righteousness can only come from Christ.

Session #8

Observe the Structure

PURPOSE OF THIS SESSION: To help us learn the steps for taking note of the structure of a passage.

FORMAT: Each person should have read "Observe the Structure" ahead of time and completed the assignment before coming. In your time together, ask if anyone has any questions about this session. As a group, help each other answer those questions. When each person feels he or she understands the concept, discuss what everyone learned through the assignment, including any questions they may have. When finished, assign Session #9 for next week.

As we travel down a path we often pass by trees along the way, and we usually don't take much notice of them. But if we stop and carefully observe them, we find that God has designed each tree to be unique. When we closely observe a tree, we find that the shape and color of the leaves and fruit, the way the branches are arranged, and the shape of the trunk are unique to each tree. These details help us learn what kind of tree it is and what its purpose is. How the parts of the tree are arranged is called the *structure* of the tree.

We find the same thing as we study individual passages of Scripture. If we read a passage quickly, we may not notice the unique ideas that God has designed the passage to teach. At first glance the passage may seem complicated and difficult to understand. But if we look closely, we find that each passage has a unique order and arrangement to its parts, much as each tree is unique in the way it's arranged.

Defining Terms: What is structure?

As we begin carefully observing the text, we take note of not only the individual words but also the major ideas and events and how they are arranged. Sometimes we see this in relationships between stories. Sometimes it's a logical progression of ideas. It's important to recognize these patterns and progressions if we're going to understand the message the author intended to give. The way the major ideas and events are arranged or organized is called the structure of the passage.

Another way of looking at structure is to think of a chain. Each section in the passage is like a link in a chain. These links may have twists and turns, but each one is connected to the others and completes the chain. Passages in the Bible are like that. Each section, like a link in a chain, is connected to the others and carries the author's ideas forward. How they are linked and how they carry his ideas forward help us understand the author's purpose.

Most passages are organized around an introductory section, which helps us see the main idea the author wants to present. This is followed by a series of sentences or sections that give detail or explain the idea. Finally, the author gives some conclusion or application. In a story this may take the form of introducing a character or setting followed by a series of events or actions leading to a climax, which is then followed by a conclusion.

Example from Genesis 1:1–2:3:

In the first chapter of Genesis, the author introduces God as the main character, and then he organizes his writing around the arrangement, or structure, of seven days. On those seven days God does a series of things that help us understand in more detail who He is and what He is about. The climax of the story is when God creates humans and gives them a purpose. There is a concluding section that describes God resting and providing all that Adam and Eve need.

With all that in mind, we might state the structure of the

passage as: An introduction to God followed by six sections detailing an increasingly complex creation, reaching a climax in the creation of people, followed by a conclusion.

Understanding the structure of the passage will not only help us understand what the author intended to say but it will also help us as we teach. We not only want to teach the same ideas as the author, but we also want to develop the ideas in our teaching the same way he arranged his ideas in the text. This session will help us learn the steps for taking note of the passage's structure.

Step #1: List the Main Ideas
As we begin to read a passage of Scripture, we should ask:

- What ideas seem most important in this passage?
- What does the author seem to emphasize?
- What are the major ideas I find as I read through the passage?

Step #2: Notice Sections
Next, look for major sections in the passage, like the major branches of a tree or links in a chain. We need to look for the transitions from one major idea or event to the next.

- Is there a shift in thought?
- Are new subjects or ideas introduced?
- Is a new scene described or a new story told?

When we do this, we need to look for patterns, such as comparisons, parallel ideas, repetitions, or steps. How does the section begin and end? Each section should contain one major idea.

Step #3: Message Statement
Once you have an idea of the major sections, write down a short title that describes the content or what is happening in

each section. These titles will help you see the major points in a passage and will help you write a message statement. The titles don't all have to be included in the message statement, but the ideas behind the titles should be.

Assignment: Study 1 Thessalonians 4:1–12

Fill out the observation/questions worksheet, keeping in mind the context of the passage. Next, go through the steps to discover the passage's structure. Write out an initial message statement for the passage, break it into sections, and then give titles to the sections, describing the content of each section. Answer the following questions to help you do that:

> ➤ What are the major ideas in this passage? (There should be one major idea for each section.)
> ➤ How would you adjust your initial message statement after looking at the structure of the passage?
> ➤ Write out a new message statement.

Application: We are often to general in application. We want to respond to God's conviction or instruction, but we aren't specific in what actions we need to take. In our busy lives it's easy to quickly forget how we were convicted. It's helpful to ask: *What steps am I going to take this week to respond to what I learned in this passage?* You may even want to ask someone to hold you accountable to take that action. As you study this week, keep your heart open to the Lord's instruction and then plan how you will respond.

Here is an example from Philippians 3:2–11:

Look out for the dogs, look out for the evildoers, look out for those who mutilate the flesh. For we are the real circumcision, who worship by the Spirit of God and glory in Christ Jesus and put no confidence in the flesh—though I myself have reason for confidence in the flesh also. If anyone else thinks he has reason for confidence in the flesh, I have more: circumcised on the eighth day, of the people of Israel, of the tribe of Benjamin, a Hebrew of Hebrews; as to the law, a Pharisee; as to zeal, a persecutor of the church; as to righteousness, under the law blameless. But whatever gain I had, I counted as a loss for the sake of Christ. Indeed, I count everything as loss because of the surpassing worth of knowing Christ Jesus my Lord. For his sake I have suffered the loss of all things and count them as rubbish, in order that I may gain Christ and be found in him, not having a righteousness of my own that comes from the law, but that which comes through faith in Christ, the righteousness from God that depends on faith—that I may know him and the power of his resurrection, and may share his sufferings, becoming like him in his death, that by any means possible I may attain the resurrection from the dead.

Major ideas:
1. Beware of those who trust in works.
2. We count our works as nothing.
3. Our goal is to be found in Christ and His righteousness.

Old Message Statement: Do not fall into thinking you have to earn your standing with God, but realize that our righteousness can only come from Christ.

New Message Statement: Don't be persuaded to trust in your works; discard them all and find your righteousness in Christ.

Session #9
Grasp the Message Flow

PURPOSE OF THIS SESSION: To learn to recognize the author's flow of ideas and purpose.

FORMAT: Each person should have read this session on "Grasp the Message Flow" ahead of time and completed the assignment before coming. In your time together, ask if anyone has any questions about this session. As a group, help each other answer those questions. When each person feels he or she understands the concept, discuss what everyone learned through the assignment, including any questions they may have. When finished, assign Session #10 for next week.

One of the most important aspects of careful Bible study is the concept of the "message flow." All writers have a sequence of ideas and a direction for those ideas. The sequence and direction are what we call the message flow. As we looked at structure, we saw that the biblical writers made major points as they wrote. These ideas are not separate ideas all by themselves. They are linked together in ways that help us understand the author's purpose. One way to picture the flow of a passage is to think of a river. The water flows down the valley.

Defining Terms: What is the "Message Flow"?

The flow of a passage may be thought of as a river of ideas. The ideas flow through the passage, one idea leading to the next. In this session we'll look at the process we go through to consider this flow of ideas and find the author's purpose.

How the author sets up the flow is partly dependent on the type of literature he's writing. If he's writing a story, or narrative, the flow is shaped by the events that take place or by the people who appear in the story. The development of the story is called the plot, or plan, of the story. For example, in the book of Jonah there's a storyline that leads us to a conclusion.

Jonah receives the word of the Lord and flees in disobedience, is confronted by the Lord in the storm and the fish, and then responds with obedience by going to preach in Nineveh, bringing about the repentance of the city. If that were the end of the story, we might conclude that the author was leading us to see that God calls us to preach to all nations in order to bring them to repentance.

However, Jonah 4 forces us to go further and see that the purpose of the story has to do with Jonah's heart and attitude. We then conclude that the author may be asking Israel (and us) to consider our hearts and whether we share God's compassion for all people. The flow of the story leads us to that conclusion.

But not all the books of the Bible are stories. Some are poetry, prophecy, or exposition. For example, the book of Ephesians is a letter to the church at Ephesus. In this type of writing there's no storyline; instead the author shapes the flow of the message by arranging a logical sequence in his writing.

He begins by mentioning all the blessings that we receive through Christ. Step by step he lays out a progression of blessings for us. Then in Ephesians 4, he begins to make practical applications that should flow out of those blessings. So we might conclude that the author's purpose in the book is that we would understand those blessings and respond in ways that honor Christ. How the book is put together, or structured, and how the ideas flow though the book lead us to that conclusion.

Individual passages of Scripture also have a flow. Sentences and paragraphs are put together in ways that lead us to the author's purpose. In an earlier session we learned about structure. We might think of the main points in each section as the stopping points along the way as we go down the river of ideas. We, the readers, are traveling down the river of ideas as we read. Each new section we come to helps us make progress toward our destination: the author's purpose for the passage.

As we are studying, we break a passage into sections, giving each section a title describing the content of that section. Next we should think about why the author wanted to say these things to the original readers. What principles or lessons did he want to give them?

Then to find the overall lesson, we think about how those ideas fit together. Where is the author taking his reader as he moves from one idea or principle to another? This is how we move from observation to understanding. We look first at *what* the author is telling us (observation) and then ask *why* the author is telling us this (understanding). As we do this for each section, we gradually build an understanding of the whole passage, concluding with: What is the overall lesson of the passage?

We look at the flow of ideas through the passage and consider how the passage ends. To what destination does this river of ideas lead us?

Original Message Statement

Remember that the message statement answers two central questions:

1. What is this passage talking about? This is called the subject of the passage and could be one word or a short phrase.

2. What is it saying about the subject? These are the things that describe or explain the subject.

We want to answer these two questions and then try to write a single complete sentence that not only states the subject but also what the passage says about that subject.

Looking at the structure and flow of a passage helps us

understand the passage well and write a good message statement. The structure helps us find the sections of the passage; the titles we write help us observe carefully the content of the sections; and then looking at the flow and answering why the author wrote each section helps us understand the author's overall purpose for the passage. Once we have described the lessons the author presented to the original readers in each section and have thought about the flow of ideas through the passage we are ready to write our message statement as applied to the original readers. We can now add these steps to the ones we had when we looked at structure.

Here is a summary of this process:

Step #1: Main Ideas: How does the passage begin? (Remember to look at the context.) What are the main ideas? Do you have questions about anything in the passage?

Step #2: Sections: What are the steps in the progress of the passage? How will you break the passage into sections, each containing a main idea? Do linking words help here?

Step #3: Titles: What ideas or lessons are taught in each section? Why were they important to the original readers? What titles would you give to these ideas?

Step #4: Flow of Ideas: What is the flow of ideas in the passage? How does each section move the author's message forward? To what conclusion does the flow of the message lead us?

Step #5: Original Message Statement: What is your original message statement?

Assignment: Study 1 Thessalonians 4:13–18
Walk through all the steps we've learned: observation,

questions, context, and structure. Then, work through the steps outlined above.

Application: We've encouraged you in this study to write down what you are discovering and thinking because it helps clarify your thoughts. This can also be true of our applications. If we write down what we think God may be asking us to do in response to His Word, it helps us clarify how we should respond. Consider what God is impressing on your heart as you study, and write down your ideas to respond more fully

Here is an example; refer back to Philippians 3:1–11:

Finally, my brothers, rejoice in the Lord....

Step #1: How does the passage begin?
Paul is urging the Philippians to rejoice and he is leading into a warning.

Step #2: What are the steps in the progress of the passage?
Paul begins by warning against the evil doers, who we learn are those who promote circumcision as a fleshly means to gain acceptance with God. He lists his accomplishments in the flesh and rejects them. He concludes by pointing to Christ and His righteousness as being far superior.

Step #3: What ideas or lessons are taught in each section? Why were they important to the original readers? What titles would you give to these ideas?
1. Beware of those who promote the flesh.
2. Our fleshly accomplishments are nothing.
3. Our whole trust is in Christ and His righteousness.

Step #4: What is the flow of ideas in the passage? How does each section move the author's message forward? To what conclusion does the flow of the message lead us?

He starts with a warning against those who promote fleshly works, shows how our works are nothing worthy, and concludes that only Christ and His works are worthy.

Step #5: What is your Message Statement?

Don't listen to those who trust in works; discard hope in

Session #10
Note the Salvation Story

PURPOSE OF THIS SESSION: To help us move from the message to the original readers to God's message for us today.

FORMAT: Each person should have read this session on "Note the Salvation Story" ahead of time and completed the assignment before coming. In your time together, ask if anyone has any questions about this session. As a group, help each other answer those questions. When each person feels he or she understands the concept, discuss what everyone learned through the assignment, including any questions they may have. When finished, assign Session #11 for next week.

So far, we've studied many tools to help us along the Bible Pathway of understanding the text of Scripture we are studying. We've learned to observe the content and structure of a passage carefully, as well as to consider the immediate context (the surrounding passages) in order to understand the passage well. We've asked good questions and thought about the flow of the message. All the while we've been thinking about a good application of the passage to our lives. Let's look once more at our Bible Pathway diagram on the next page and note where the "Bible's Salvation Story" appears.

Bible Pathway

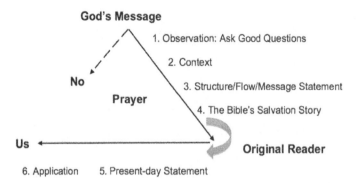

God's Message

1. Observation: Ask Good Questions

2. Context

No

3. Structure/Flow/Message Statement

Prayer

4. The Bible's Salvation Story

Us ← ———————————— **Original Reader**

6. Application   5. Present-day Statement

Defining Terms: What is the "Salvation Story"?

The Bible's salvation story helps us move from the message to the original readers to God's message for us today. The Bible is made up of sixty-six books containing many stories, songs, poems, and letters; but in another sense, it's one book with one large story. The Bible's salvation story looks at this bigger story and considers how each part fits into the whole. Ultimately, it's the story of God's purpose to progressively reveal Himself to people, redeem us through Christ, and restore our relationship with Him. All of the stories in the Bible lead us step by step toward that purpose. The Bible's salvation story teaches us to consider how each passage of Scripture fits in with the overall story of the Bible—something we need to consider when we are studying any passage of Scripture. Another way to say that is to consider how each passage of Scripture relates to the gospel.

Throughout our study we've emphasized the need to understand what the author was saying to the original reader before we try to apply God's message to our lives. We will not fully understand the message to the original reader until we understand the portion of the salvation story that precedes it, whether in the Old Testament or New.

The salvation story that precedes any passage we look at forms part of the context. We've learned that every passage has a flow of ideas in it. This is also true of the larger story of the Bible. We must try to determine what purpose the passage we are studying plays in the overall flow of the Bible's message.

Consider this example: When you begin reading a new novel, you don't begin randomly in the middle of the book. If you did, you wouldn't understand that part of the story. It's not that you can't understand the language. The problem is that you wouldn't know the context of that scene. You wouldn't know the characters or how the story has developed to that point.

Reading the Bible is somewhat like that. If we're going to fully understand the meaning of any passage, we need to understand its relationship with the rest of the story. Every passage in the Bible has other passages that precede it and that introduce characters. These earlier passages also teach principles and ideas that form a basis for what the present passage is teaching. We need to be aware of this as we consider the meaning of any passage we study.

There's one more thing that's unique and important to remember about the Bible. It is a true story about life from the beginning of creation to the beginning of the new creation, which will come at the end of time. It gives us perspective on what has come before us, on our lives now, and on what will happen in the future.

We stand in the New Testament age looking back at biblical history and view it from our position in Christ. The original readers looked at what was written from the viewpoint of their own time and place. They could look back over what had been written before their time, but they didn't have a full understanding of the rest of the story. We can see much more of the story because we are nearer the end.

This again is somewhat like reading a novel. As we read the first few chapters, we understand the drift of the story. But when we finish the book, we can look back and see more clearly how those first chapters fit into the story, and we also understand the author's purpose more fully.

We always want to begin with the author's intent for the

original readers. But then, in light of the Bible's salvation story, we must look at the passage from our perspective as New Testament believers and ask what message God now has for us. How the passage fits within the accumulating message of the gospel as it develops through Scripture will help us determine that. The following diagram illustrates this.

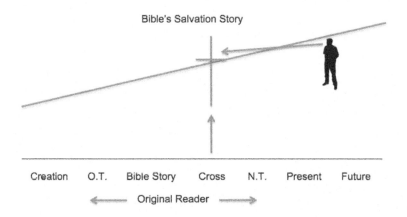

This illustrates that throughout biblical history, God has been slowly revealing His salvation plan. Each passage in the Bible adds to or reinforces the principles of the salvation story. Gradually, God reveals more and more of His plan to redeem His people (bring them back into relationship with Him) through Jesus Christ.

At the beginning of the Bible, in Genesis, we see very little of the salvation story, but more and more of it is revealed throughout the Old Testament. By the time Jesus came, He could show many, many passages in the Old Testament that pointed to Himself (Luke 24:25–27). The New Testament goes on to explain much of the story and to point forward to some parts that are not yet finished.

It's particularly important to see the movement from the old covenant in the Old Testament to the new covenant in the New Testament (a covenant is an agreement between two parties). God originally made a covenant with Abraham. This covenant was a promise to bless him and through him all nations and was unconditional as a result of God's grace.

The entire story of Abraham teaches us that one enters this covenant by faith. Later, God made a covenant with Israel at Mount Sinai (Exodus 34:27). The book of Hebrews calls this the old covenant (Hebrews 8:6). The essence of the old covenant was that if Israel obeyed God's law, He would bless them. If they disobeyed His law, God would curse and judge them. Because the Israelites, like all of us, were sinners by nature, they always broke God's law. The purpose of this covenant was to teach Israel not to depend upon their own works for salvation and blessing but to pursue them by faith. The old covenant did not replace the Abrahamic covenant; it pointed them to Abraham's faith and ultimately to Christ. The following diagram illustrates these principles.

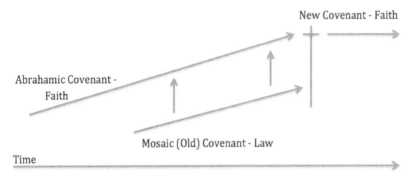

God promised Israel a new covenant (Jeremiah 31:31). The essence of the new covenant is that God blesses us on account of His Son, but we must place our trust in Him. This covenant restates God's covenant with Abraham and it's the covenant that we as Christians live under. We enter this covenant the same way Abraham did, by God's grace through faith. When we look at the Old Testament, we must remember that we are not under the old covenant and the law as Israel was. We are under the new covenant, which fulfills the law and was intended to point us to Christ. We are now in Christ with all the benefits of forgiveness, justification, and the presence of the Holy Spirit.

We must take into account this significant transition when we try to understand the message God has for us in Old Testament passages. The salvation story has its ultimate fulfillment in the gospel (the good news of life through Christ and in Christ, not based on good works on our part). The message for us in Old Testament passages will ultimately be related to the gospel as well.

Assignment: Study 1 Thessalonians 5:1–11
Study 1 Thessalonians 5:1–11 using all the tools and steps we've learned. This passage talks about things that will happen in the future. Think carefully about what God's message through Paul, Timothy, and Silvanus was to the Thessalonians. Then think about the ideas presented earlier in the Bible that form a foundation or context for this passage. As you do, think about the Old Testament passages that form a background for what the authors say here. For example, what is the Old Testament background for "the day of the Lord"? (It may be helpful to use a tool, such as biblegateway.com, to look up uses of "the day of the Lord" in the Old Testament. Make sure you put the phrase in quotes to search.) How does that help us understand this passage better?

Application: Make sure that the application you make this week leads you to depend upon and rejoice in Jesus more and more, and make sure it is founded on the gospel. Trust in Christ to help you obey and thank Him for His grace that enables us to be in fellowship with Him. Remember to thank Him for the hope we have in Him.

Here is an example from Philippians 3:1-11:

Finally, my brothers, rejoice in the Lord. To write the same things to you is no trouble to me and is safe for you
Look out for the dogs, look out for the evildoers, look out for those who mutilate the flesh. For we are the real circumcision, who worship by the Spirit of God and glory in Christ Jesus and put no confidence in the flesh—though I myself have reason for confidence in the flesh also. If anyone else thinks he has reason for confidence in the flesh, I have more: circumcised on the eighth day, of the people of Israel, of the tribe of Benjamin, a Hebrew of Hebrews; as to the law, a Pharisee; as to zeal, a persecutor of the church; as to righteousness, under the law blameless. But whatever gain I had, I counted as a loss for the sake of Christ. Indeed, I count everything as loss because of the surpassing worth of knowing Christ Jesus my Lord. For his sake I have suffered the loss of all things and count them as rubbish, in order that I may gain Christ and be found in him, not having a righteousness of my own that comes from the law, but that which comes through faith in Christ, the righteousness from God that depends on faith—that I may know him and the power of his resurrection, and may share his sufferings, becoming like him in his death, that by any means possible I may attain the resurrection from the dead.

Salvation Story: Without understanding the Old Testament practice of circumcision it is hard to understand this passage. Because this was a much bigger problem in Paul's day than it is in ours, we must think of similar issues that cause us to trust in ourselves rather than in Christ alone. Baptism may be one modern issue that some trust in rather than in Christ alone.

Session #11
Ponder the Application

PURPOSE OF THIS SESSION: To learn what it means to apply a Scripture passage to our lives.

FORMAT: Each person should have read this session on "Ponder the Application" ahead of time and completed the assignment. In your time together, answer any questions anyone has about this concept. When each person feels he or she understands the concept, discuss what everyone learned through the assignment, including any questions they may have. When finished, assign Session #12 for next week.

The last step in Careful Bible Study is applying what we have studied to our lives. If we neglect this part of Bible study, we fail to profit from all the work we've done.

Defining Terms: What should we apply?
Sometimes we're tempted to think that application is natural and doesn't require much effort if we've worked hard on understanding the passage. But application takes work too, and if we think that what God has said is important, then how we apply His Word is equally important. In fact, the whole purpose of our study is to discover what God has said so we can carefully apply that to our lives. So we want to work as hard on our applications as we do on our study.

We will need the Holy Spirit's help with application just as much as we need His help with our study. Don't rush to application before you've finished the other steps.

God's Word itself gives us some guidance in how to apply Scripture in 2 Timothy 3:16–17, which says: "All Scripture is breathed out by God and profitable for *teaching*, for *reproof*, for *correction* and for *training in righteousness*, that the man of God may be competent, equipped for every good work" (emphasis mine).

These four purposes can be thought of as a guideline for how we should apply the Word to our lives. In our study we are careful to understand what the Word *teaches*, asking, "What pathway has God laid out for my life?" Then we need to ask, "How am I not walking in that pathway?" That's what's meant by *reproof*. Next ask, "What changes does God want me to make to move me toward His pathway?" That's *correction*. Finally, "What steps am I going to take to move toward His pathway?" Making changes *trains* us to walk righteously. The following "Four-Question Process" can help you think through this.

"teaching": What's *right* in God's Word? What does this passage teach about God and His will for my life? What pathway has He laid out for me to follow Him? (Make a list of what you've learned from this passage.)

"for rebuking": What's *wrong* (lacking) in my life compared to this? What am I being convicted about? How have I moved from His pathway?

"for correction": What should I *do*? What does the Spirit want me to do differently in response to this? What changes must I make to get on God's pathway for my life?

"training in righteousness": *How* and *when* will I *do* it? What specific steps do I need to take to move toward God's pathway? When will I do this? Who will I share this with?

As we think about the four questions, we should recognize that Scripture calls us to change in several different ways. Sometimes we need to *think* differently or have a different attitude. Sometimes we need to *do* something different, either starting some new activity or work, adjusting what we do, or stopping some action or activity in our lives. Sometimes what we *love* needs to change. Often it's a combination of these things that God wants to do in our lives. We must seek the Holy Spirit's help in thinking about the different ways that He wants us to change and in finding and implementing a good plan for working on them.

The final step in the process of developing a good application requires us to think carefully about the gospel. No lasting change in our lives is possible apart from Christ. Jesus reminds us of this in John 15:3-5. Notice that in verse 3 He says that we are clean; we are washed through His sacrifice so that we are acceptable before God, even with our continuing struggles in life. The good news of the gospel is that we are saved by grace through faith in Jesus Christ. That's our foundation and encouragement.

We will not be "more saved" if we make the changes in our life that the Scripture is pointing us toward, but we will be more fruitful. His character will be more evident in our lives as we depend on Him and are then changed to be more like Him. This is also part of the good news. The central point of the John 15 passage is that only by abiding in Him can we bear fruit.

This will not happen just because we try harder or are more disciplined. It will come through Him by grace and the work of the Holy Spirit. So, we must always come back to the gospel and find our hope and help in Christ through the sanctifying work of the Holy Spirit. We're reminded that apart from Him, we can do nothing (John 15:5). Our applications should encourage us that because of the gospel we can depend upon the Spirit to help us obey God's Word.

The Aim of the Passage
One important aspect of application has to do with the aim of the passage. By *aim*, we mean the application the author intended for the original readers. It's important for us to think about that because the aim God had for them will be consistent with the aim He has for us. In the Old Testament there will be differences between the application to them and

the one to us because they were under the old covenant and we are under the new covenant. But the aim of the text for them will be parallel to the aim for us.

For example, in the book of Leviticus there are hundreds of laws given to Israel covering a wide range of issues in life. The aim of this book was to teach Israel that everything in their lives was to be done in relation to the holiness of God. If they kept these laws, they would be living in right relationship to Him. When we read Leviticus, the aim is the same for us. We are also to live our lives in relation to God's holiness. But the difference is that we've learned we cannot do that through the law. We must live out our lives by faith in Christ to live in right relationship with God and His holiness.

In the New Testament the aim of the text to the original readers will also be parallel with the aim for us. We only need to account for the differences in culture and circumstances. For example, 1 Corinthians 8 teaches about eating food offered to idols. The aim of the passage was to teach the Corinthians that there is nothing wrong with eating meat that was sacrificed to idols, because we know the idols are not really gods. But if some do not have that knowledge or strength of faith, our eating might cause them to stumble by encouraging them to eat against their consciences. Therefore, we should not eat this meat if it causes our brothers or sisters to stumble.

In our culture, we don't encounter this issue, since we are not offered meat that was offered to idols. So do we just skip a passage like this because the cultural situation is different from the first century? Certainly not! If we did, we would be missing some important lessons from Scripture that apply to Christians who live in any time. So, how do we apply this message to our lives?

In our day there are habits or activities that might cause someone, particularly someone who is weak in their faith, to stumble. How do we make our decisions on these matters? Paul teaches that the faith of weaker brothers and sisters is more important than our own individual freedoms. What a message for today! We live in an age where people, including

Christians, are totally into their own rights and freedoms, but God has given the church a different set of values. Do we make our decisions about these things based only on what we feel is right and wrong? Or do we consider how our actions may tempt others to violate their consciences?

The aim of the passage is not about the particular activity itself but about the decision-making we do. Our application may vary in particulars, but it should follow the aim of the text in principle. As you ponder applications, think about the Four-Question process and about the aim of the text. If you do both well, you will have wise, specific, and biblically accurate applications that will equip you to thrive as a godly person.

Assignment: Study 1 Thessalonians 5:12–28
Study this passage using all the tools and steps you've learned.

Application: Use the Four-Question Process to determine the application God wants you to focus on this week. Keep in mind the aim of the text as you do so. Jesus said, "apart from me you can do nothing" (John 15:5). Make sure the application you make leads you to depend upon and rejoice in Jesus more and more and is, therefore, founded on the gospel. Try to write out your application in a single sentence. We call this our "Application Statement."

Here is an example from Philippians 3:1–11:

Finally, my brothers, rejoice in the Lord. To write the same things to you is no trouble to me and is safe for you

Look out for the dogs, look out for the evildoers, look out for those who mutilate the flesh. For we are the real circumcision, who worship by the Spirit of God and glory in Christ Jesus and put no confidence in the flesh—though I myself have reason for confidence in the flesh also. If anyone else thinks he has reason for confidence in the flesh, I have more: circumcised on the eighth day, of the people of Israel, of the tribe of Benjamin, a Hebrew of Hebrews; as to the law, a Pharisee; as to zeal, a persecutor of the church; as to righteousness, under the law blameless. But whatever gain I had, I counted as a loss for the sake of Christ. Indeed, I count everything as loss because of the surpassing worth of knowing Christ Jesus my Lord. For his sake I have suffered the loss of all things and count them as rubbish, in order that I may gain Christ and be found in him, not having a righteousness of my own that comes from the law, but that which comes through faith in Christ, the righteousness from God that depends on faith—that I may know him and the power of his resurrection, and may share his sufferings, becoming like him in his death, that by any means possible I may attain the resurrection from the dead.

Four-Question Process:
Teaching: Don't fall into the natural habit of trying to earn my way into God's favor.
Rebuking: Examine what I am trying to add to salvation in Christ alone. Am I entertaining any hope in myself or my performance?
Correction: Move away from using my performance as a way to please God.
Training in Righteousness: This week I am going to remind myself each morning to remember that I am not accepted based on my performance but on Christ's righteousness.

Session #12
Review

PURPOSE OF THIS SESSION: To review what we've learned in this study.

FORMAT: Discuss the passage you studied, which you completed on your own before coming to the group session, and come to a consensus as to what the book of 1 Thessalonians is about. Then read through this "Review" and discuss anything from past weeks you have questions about.

Let's look again at all the steps in our Bible Pathway diagram. Is there any part of this that you would like to discuss further?

Bible Pathway

God's Message

1. Observation: Ask Good Questions

2. Context

3. Structure/Flow/Message Statement

4. The Bible's Salvation Story

No

Prayer

Us

Original Reader

6. Application   5. Present-day Statement

Hopefully you've enjoyed gaining insight into the passages that you've studied and have made some good applications to your life. Having gone through this study will also make you more discerning as you listen to others teach. But remember, these methods will only help you if you use them in a disciplined manner. It takes practice and repetition to develop the habit of good Bible study.

We strongly suggest that you either continue with this small group in further studying God's Word or join another Bible study that uses this method. This will help you consolidate your understanding and strengthen your skills for future study. If you have the courage to start another study and teach this method to others, it will not only help them but will help you more fully grasp the tools and method as well. The person teaching usually learns more than the students he or she teaches.

We have presented the basic tools and process for study. But not all Scripture is the same type of literature. Some parts require special tools to study well. Some of those tools are provided in the addendum. Hopefully this will help you continue to learn to study as you move on from the New Testament epistles to other books in the Bible.

Our ultimate desire is that all God's people all over the world understand the Bible. We know that unless they learn to study well, they will never understand all of His Word. Thank you for your efforts to learn. Please consider what role God may want you to take in spreading these skills to other believers around you. May God be glorified as we work together to spread the knowledge of His Word and, therefore, the gospel of Jesus Christ to all people.

Assignment: Summarize 1 Thessalonians
Ponder what you think the entire book is about. What did Paul most want to communicate through this book?

Addendum

Types of literature

As we become familiar with the Bible, we soon recognize that there are many different types of writings in it. Sometimes we find stories, such as in the book of Jonah. In other places there are letters, such as the ones Paul wrote to Timothy. We also find poetry in many books, especially the Psalms. The Bible also includes prophetic writing, such as in Isaiah; proverbs, as in the book of Proverbs; law, as in Leviticus; and apocalyptic writing in books like Revelation.

It's common for individual books to contain several of these types of literature. For example, although the book of Jonah is one large story, chapter two is written as poetry. Within these different types of writing, there are variations as well. There are several types of stories in the Bible. Some are primarily a recounting of historical events. Others, such as Jonah, are historical but designed to make a theological point. Some stories in the Bible are fictional, such as many of the parables that Jesus taught. In these, Jesus created the story to make a central point to His audience. The book of Job is a story mostly written in poetic form. The Gospels are a series of interconnected stories that introduce us to Jesus and explain who He was and what He did.

As we study the Bible, we must be careful to take into account the type of writing we are reading. Each type of writing requires unique approaches to interpretation. We will make mistakes in understanding God's purpose in each passage if we treat them all the same. For example, we cannot treat proverbs in the same way we do the commandments of the law. That's because the proverbs encourage wisdom while the commands of the law require obedience.

Basic tools, such as good observation, asking questions, context, and structure are all important in studying any part of Scripture. But we also need to be wise in considering God's purpose in using a variety of types of literature to communicate His message to us. This will help us better understand His message to us so we can better apply it to our lives.

Here are some principles you can use in interpreting each type of literature.

Stories (narrative)

As with all Scripture, we need to ask what the author's purpose for the story was. Why did he tell this story the way he did? We need to ask if the story is given to provide historical context or if there is a specific point to the story. Also, we need to look carefully at how the story is connected to other stories around it to find clues to its purpose and meaning. It's usually helpful to ask what the story tells us about God, who is generally the main character, before we ask what it tells us about people or ourselves. Remember that stories usually are not normative; that is, they are not meant to tell us how to live. They often give examples of people's failures or of a specific course of action in a particular time and place. We should look for the principles taught in the story and then think how they apply to us in our time.

Some stories, like the parables, are fictional. They are usually given to illustrate or make one general point. We should avoid allegorizing or finding meaning in each part of the story. Instead, we should look for the central lesson taught.

In many stories, such as in the Gospels, what precedes the story and what follows is very important in understanding the story's meaning. Context becomes especially important in these situations.

The letters (epistles)

Remember that the letters were written to a certain reader or group of readers in a particular time and place in history. We need to always consider what the author intended to say to them before we ask how it applies to us. How the sections of the letter are linked together and the flow of ideas or sequence of thought are important to understanding the author's intent. Perhaps more than in any other type of writing, to understand an epistle we should consider each word and how it's used in a sentence.

Poetry and wisdom literature

It's important to remember that poetry is often figurative and uses graphic terms to communicate deep feelings. Often we should not take what is written literally but consider what feelings the author intended by the terms he has used. In contrast to the Psalms, the wisdom literature in Job, Ecclesiastes, Song of Songs, and Lamentations should be understood in the context of the whole book.

For example, in Job we often have a lot of false thinking expressed, especially by Job's "friends." It's the overall story that has meaning. We should avoid looking at individual verses out of context in these stories. We should also avoid allegorizing in books like the Song of Songs. The highly figurative language that is used there has symbolic value. But not every term or illustration has specific theological meaning.

Be careful about seeing the Proverbs as promises or commands. The Holy Spirit inspired general statements of truth designed to teach us wisdom. So we need to ask what we can learn about wise behavior or thinking rather than what we should necessarily obey.

It's interesting that the Psalms are the most quoted Old Testament book by the New Testament authors, and most of those references are about Christ. The writers of the Psalms miraculously prophesied about Jesus hundreds of years before His birth. The simplest way to figure these references out is to see how Christ and the New Testament authors understood them. See, for instance, Psalm 110:1 and Matthew 22:44.

Law and commands

Throughout the Bible we find commands that God has given

us. Commands are always meant to call a person to obedience. But we must remember that not all of the commands were given directly to us. The Old Testament commands in the law were given to Israel and intended to ultimately teach them (and us) that they could not be justified before God by obedience. The commands were given to expose sin.

In the New Testament we're told that we're not under the law but under grace. So we should remember two things. First, we are not under any of the commands of the Old Testament law. That doesn't mean they are bad, just that they're not meant for us to obey. Their purpose has been fulfilled.

Second, even though we are under grace, it doesn't mean that we are not called to obedience. Instead, we are given many commands in the New Testament. The difference is that our obedience does not gain our justification (right standing) before God. Rather our obedience is a product of that justification, which is by faith in Jesus. Be careful not to pick and choose between which Old Testament commands we are to obey. We can learn about sin, about ourselves, and about God in them, but they were not given as law for us. At the same time the commands of the New Testament are not just suggestions; God intends for us to obey them. Often they restate or continue the commands of the Old Testament. But we also must remember that the power for obedience comes through faith in Christ and the power of the Spirit (Galatians 5:16), and that our justification is found by faith in Him, not in our perfect obedience.

Prophecy
It's helpful to remember that prophecy is not always about the future. Often prophecy spoke about the future of ancient Israel, which is now in the past for us. Sometimes it points to the first coming of Christ, which was accomplished 2,000 years ago when Jesus was born, died, and resurrected. At other times prophecy speaks about things still future to us. The key is to ask to whom the author was writing and what

was his purpose.

Prophecy is primarily about God and His hatred of sin as well as His grace, forgiveness, and glory. From the prophets we can learn a lot about God and His character and purposes, and about our need for His grace. We can also learn about what angers God and how He disciplines, as well as how gracious He is. The things the prophets wrote about that are still future to us are probably as much a mystery to us as the other prophecies were to ancient Israel. We should be careful about how specific we are in detailing what we think they teach about the future.

Apocalyptic Writing

Apocalyptic writing, such as in Daniel and Revelation, is a combination of prophecy and poetic or figurative language. Again, as with poetry, we should be careful not to draw specific conclusions from every figure of speech or symbol. Rather, our goal is to understand the overall message. That message is always related to God and His sovereignty, His hatred of sin, and His grace toward His people. Rather than being frightened by what we find in this literature, we should be encouraged about God's final and complete victory on behalf of His people.

Apocalyptic literature is full of symbolic language. The authors use imagery to describe or teach us about things that were to come or will yet come in the future. Much of what God revealed to the authors is hard for them to describe because it's greater than words alone can state. Using metaphor and symbolism helps them write about what these things are like. If we miss this, we may be in danger of taking literally what the author meant to be illustrative, and we may miss his real point.

When approaching a book like Revelation, we shouldn't focus on the dates, figures of speech, and the timing of future events. That might cause us to miss the grand vision of God as holy, just, and all-powerful, along with the certainty of His glorious final victory over evil and how He will gather His people. Focus on what we learn about God, His triumph, and His general plan for the future, as well as the glories of His kingdom. Celebrate that no matter what we go through, He will reign in glory forever and we will be with Him!

Parables

A parable is a type of story that often occurs in the Gospels. Parables are figurative stories that use everyday situations to convey a spiritual truth. Jesus often used this type of story when He encountered opposition from the religious authorities. While they were intended to teach spiritual lessons to His followers, they were also intended to hide those lessons from the hardhearted people who rejected Him (Mark 4:10–12).

Like all stories, it's important to consider the context of the parable as we try to understand it. Often the introduction or the conclusion to the parable will help us understand it. Sometimes Jesus Himself explains the lesson. In many cases understanding the stories or dialogues that surround the parable helps us catch the meaning. As we study, we should remember that parables were usually intended to teach *one main point.* Parables are not allegories (where every person or element is symbolic of something specific). Not every detail in them has spiritual significance.

In the parables we should look for the main point and try to understand why Jesus told the story. Looking at the passages that come before and after the parable can help us understand the purpose that the biblical author had in placing the story where he did. Remember that the author's purpose may be slightly different from Jesus' purpose. Jesus had a purpose for teaching the parable, but the biblical author may have had additional purposes in presenting the parable in the context that he did. He may have wanted to teach us something about Jesus as well as about what Jesus taught.

If you would like to, do the following exercise in Mark 4 to further understand the purpose of parables.

Exercise

Study Mark 4 according to the structure of the passage.

1. Jesus tells a parable in Mark 4:1–9. Complete an observation/questions sheet for this parable. What do you conclude is the main point?

2. Jesus tells His disciples why He taught in parables in Mark 4:10–13. What was Jesus' explanation?

3. Jesus explains the parable in Mark 4:13–20. What do you now think is the main point? How does this fit the context in Mark? What is the structure of the parable, and how does that impact our understanding of the main idea? How would the lesson of this parable apply to our lives today?

4. Jesus comments on revelation in Mark 4:21–25. Why does He make these comments here? What is His point?

Seeing Christ in the Old Testament

As believers under a new covenant, one of our central purposes in understanding the Bible is to encounter Jesus Christ and to understand the gospel. But how do we properly see Christ in the Old Testament passages? We cannot simply impose Christ onto the passage. This exercise leads you through the steps to seeing Christ in and Old Testament passage without going above the line. Look again at our Bible Pathway diagram.

Bible Pathway

God's Message

1. Observation: Ask Good Questions

2. Context

No

3. Structure/Flow/Message Statement

Prayer

4. The Bible's Salvation Story

Us ←

Original Reader

6. Application   5. Present-day Statement

As we look at any passage of Scripture, our first concern is to understand the intent of the author's message to the original readers. His intent is never to teach them directly about Jesus Christ, because Jesus is never mentioned by name in the Old Testament. Many passages point to Him using other terms, such as the seed of the woman, the seed of Abraham, the prophet who will be like Moses, the Son of David, the coming king, the Messiah, etc. The author's intent in each passage was to point his readers to the person mentioned: the seed, the prophet, and the coming King. When we study these passages, we must first find the author's intent for the original reader. We go through the steps in our diagram to arrive at that conclusion. But we do not insert Jesus into the original message statement at this point because He is not named in the text given to the original reader. We understand that the Bible was pointing people to the coming seed, or King, or whatever the passage mentions, but we must first understand what the passage was saying to the original readers.

After we have seen the message to the original readers, we must look at the Salvation Story and ask, "What does this passage teach us about Jesus or the gospel?" Looking at the Salvation Story helps us move toward a New Covenant understanding. This is where we begin to consider Christ or the gospel. We can begin to see how Jesus fulfilled the promise of the seed, or prophet, etc. If the figure of Christ is not present, we can understand the fact that in Him, through the gospel, we have something much better than those under the old covenant had under the law. (This is explained clearly by the writer of the Book of Hebrews.)

In terms of our diagram, we do not bring Jesus into the diagram on the right-hand side. We introduce Him as we move toward the bottom of the diagram, toward our present-day statement and application. Understanding the Salvation Story helps us move toward that message and application. If we insert Christ into our understanding on the right side of the diagram as we are discussing the text as given to the original readers, we will go above the line and say more than the text says. But when we introduce Christ through the Salvation Story, we are fulfilling the ultimate purpose of the passage and finding appropriate application for our lives.

Examples

Look at Isaiah 53. How should we understand this text? If we simply begin by saying that this text is about Jesus Christ, we are saying more than the text is saying because it does not tell us that the person described is Jesus. We only know that this is about Christ as a result of our understanding of the Salvation Story.

We can begin by thinking about how Isaiah prophesied about a coming person who would suffer on behalf or God's people. We can point out the various things that the passage says about that person. Then we can explain how Jesus fulfilled all of these prophecies.

Isaiah 53 is pretty simple, because we understand the text as written to the original readers and then consider how the New Testament shows this person is Jesus Christ. Not all passages in the Old Testament are this easy to understand. Think about the book of Jonah. Christ is not mentioned in the book, and there is not even the mention of a Christ-type figure. So, how do we see Christ or the gospel in the book?

Some insert the gospel into the message that Jonah preached to the Ninevites. But that is going above the line because Jonah's message was one of judgment, not a message offering forgiveness through repentance and faith.

In Jonah we learn that God has a right to be merciful to anyone He wants to, even to people as terrible as the Ninevites. We also learn that He wants His people to share His heart of compassion for all the lost. These principles point us toward Christ and the gospel. It is because of the work of Christ on the cross that God can be just and merciful to any sinner, no matter how bad they are. Because we share in His mercy through faith in Christ, we should also have compassion on other sinners around us and share the message of repentance, faith, and salvation with them. As we study Jonah, we do not say Jonah was a picture of Christ, nor do we say he was preaching the gospel to the Ninevites. But we *can* say we should be different from Jonah and share God's heart for the lost. Because we know the full Salvation Story and have experienced God's grace, we should share the gospel message of salvation through faith in Jesus with all sinners.

Leader's Questions

If you are using the *Pathways Bible Study Method* in a group setting, the following questions will be useful to get discussion going and to make sure everyone in the group understands each tool introduced. These are to be used after everyone in the group has completed the lesson.

Session #1
Questions concerning "The Bible Pathway"
- ➤ In what way is Bible study like walking on a path?
- ➤ What wrong paths do you feel you've been on in the past as you've studied the Bible?
- ➤ What does it mean that the Bible "was not written *to* us, but it was written *for* us"?
- ➤ Why is it so important to understand what God's message was to the original readers?
- ➤ An example in this session is the Old Testament command to sacrifice animals. Can you think of any other examples that illustrate that the Bible was not written to us but was written for us?
- ➤ Do you have any questions about the "Bible Pathway" illustration at the end of Session #1?

Questions concerning the assignment
1 Thessalonians:
- ➤ As you read 1 Thessalonians, who are the original readers?
- ➤ Did you find the Thessalonians mentioned anywhere else in Scripture?
- ➤ Can you guess why this was book was written to the original readers?
1 Thessalonians 1:
- ➤ What do you think the author meant to say to his people in this chapter?

➤ How do you think he wanted them to apply this message to their lives?
➤ Is the application any different for you?

Session #2

Questions concerning "Careful Bible Study"

- ➢ Why is prayer so essential in our study of the Bible?
- ➢ According to this session, what are the three steps of Careful Bible Study?
- ➢ What does it mean to carefully, rather than casually, read?
- ➢ If you can disagree with someone's observation, it has moved onto understanding. Why is it so important than we refrain from moving too quickly to understanding?
- ➢ How can you learn to prayerfully think or meditate on a passage of Scripture?
- ➢ Why is it so important to consider how the passage fits into the rest of the Bible?
- ➢ Why is it important to recognize that application isn't always an action but can also address what we think or how we love?

Questions concerning the assignment

1 Thessalonians 1:

- ➢ What new insights did you gain by studying this chapter again?
- ➢ What important, repeated, surprising, or hard to understand words or phrases did you note?
- ➢ How were the ideas connected?
- ➢ What were the author's main points?
- ➢ Is there anything you've read or studied this week that made you realize your life is not fully in harmony with God, His character, and His thoughts?

Session #3

Questions concerning "Ask Good Questions"

- ➤ Why is asking good questions so essential to understanding a passage?
- ➤ Does asking *who, what, where, when, why,* and *how* help you get a better grasp on the author's intent? Explain.
- ➤ How might the author's choice of words give us clues as to what he wants us to get out of the passage?
- ➤ Was it helpful to use the columns of observations and questions? Why or why not?

Questions concerning the assignment

1 Thessalonians 1:

- ➤ What observations did you make this week?
- ➤ What questions came to mind as you thought about what you observed?
- ➤ Over the last three weeks of looking at this passage, what most stands out to you and why?
- ➤ Are you aware of any way the Lord is prompting you to change your actions as a result of your study?

Session #4

Questions concerning "Read in Context"

- ➤ How is reading in context similar to living in community?
- ➤ Why is it so important to consider the context of the passage?
- ➤ How do the previous passages influence your understanding of the passage you are currently reading?
- ➤ Why should we consider the passages that lie ahead of what we are reading?
- ➤ What does that tell us about the importance of reading the entire book when we are studying a passage within it?
- ➤ Words closer to the passage have a larger bearing on its meaning than those farther away. Is there ever an instance when that is not necessarily true? If so, explain.

Questions concerning the assignment

1 Thessalonians 2:1–12:

- ➤ What did you observe from this passage?
- ➤ What questions came to mind as you studied?
- ➤ How did 1 Thessalonians 1 influence how you thought about this passage?
- ➤ Did you have a chance to look ahead to 1 Thessalonians 3? If so, what insight did it give you into your study of chapter 2?
- ➤ Is there anything you learned this week that points out how your thinking needs to change? How can you grow to think more like Christ?

Session #5

Questions concerning "Recognize Preunderstanding & Stay on the Line"

- ➤ What preunderstandings have colored your view of the Bible?
- ➤ What passages seem so familiar that you assume you know what they mean without studying it carefully?
- ➤ Are you aware of how strongly your theological convictions govern how you look at a text? Give an example of a passage that you've dismissed because it doesn't fit your theological framework.
- ➤ Why is it important to keep in mind that our understanding is always partial and imperfect?
- ➤ How can we be better prepared to subject our understanding to what the text actually says?
- ➤ How can you be more submissive, dependent, and disciplined as you study the Bible?
- ➤ When have you been tempted to go "above the line" and add things to Scripture?
- ➤ When have you been tempted to go "below the line" and explain away something the Bible says?

Questions concerning the assignment

1 Thessalonians 2:13–20:

- ➤ What did you observe from this passage?
- ➤ What questions came to mind as you studied?
- ➤ What understanding did you gain?
- ➤ Were you aware of any preunderstanding that affected the way you've always looked at this text?
- ➤ Is there anything you encountered in your study this week that may indicate you need to change or refine your beliefs?

Session #6

Questions concerning "Notice Linking Words"

> ➤ Why is it so important that we notice linking words in a passage?
>
> ➤ How do linking words give us clues as to the true meaning of a text?
>
> ➤ Explain how linking words help us see the *reason for* or *result of* what is said in a passage.

Questions concerning the assignment

1 Thessalonians 3:1–5:

> ➤ What did you observe from this passage?
>
> ➤ What questions came to mind as you studied?
>
> ➤ What understanding did you gain?
>
> ➤ What linking words did you notice?
>
> ➤ How did those linking words help you understand the passage better?
>
> ➤ Did you notice anything from this passage that caused you to ask God to redirect the affections of your heart to match His?

Session #7

Questions concerning "Write a Message Statement"

> ➤ How does a message statement help you understand the meaning of a passage?
> ➤ A message statement forces us to consider what the passage is about and what it's saying on the subject. How might reflecting on those two things help you in writing a message statement?
> ➤ A message statement should not be over sixteen words. Why is it important that we keep it concise?
> ➤ What did you learn from the example in 1 Timothy 5:1–2?
> ➤ What did you learn from the example in James 1:2–8?

Questions concerning the assignment

1 Thessalonians 3:6–13:

> ➤ What did you observe from this passage?
> ➤ What questions came to mind as you studied?
> ➤ What understanding did you gain?
> ➤ What does the context tell you?
> ➤ Did you notice any linking words?
> ➤ What was your message statement?
> ➤ What is the most significant thing God impressed on you in this passage?

Session #8

Questions concerning "Observe the Structure"

- How is the structure of a passage similar to the structure of a tree?
- How is it similar to the links of a chain?
- What did you learn from the example in Genesis 1:1–2:3?
- How does listing the main ideas of a passage help us understand its structure?
- How does noticing the passage's sections further our understanding of its structure?
- Why is understanding the structure of a passage vital in coming up with a message statement?

Questions concerning the assignment

1 Thessalonians 4:1–12:

- What did you observe from this passage?
- What questions came to mind as you studied?
- What are the major ideas in this passage?
- How would you adjust your initial message statement after looking at the structure of this passage?
- What is your new message statement?
- What steps are you going to take to respond to what you learned in this passage?

Session #9

Questions concerning "Grasp the Message Flow"

 ➤ Why is it important to understand the message flow of a passage?
 ➤ How does the type of literature a writer is using affect the message flow? Give an example.
 ➤ How does each new section help us grasp the message flow?
 ➤ How does grasping the message flow help us in writing a message statement?
 ➤ Is there anything you don't understand about the message flow?

Questions concerning the assignment

1 Thessalonians 4:13–18:

 ➤ What did you observe from this passage?
 ➤ What questions came to mind as you studied?
 ➤ What is the purpose of each section?
 ➤ How does each section move the author's message along?
 ➤ How did you title each section?
 ➤ What is your new message statement considering these titles?
 ➤ What ideas did you write down concerning how you can apply this passage?

Session #10

Questions concerning "Note the Salvation Story"

- ➤ Very briefly, how would you define the Bible's salvation story?
- ➤ Why is it so important that we keep this story in mind as we study the Bible?
- ➤ How do all the stories in the Bible center on the central salvation story?
- ➤ How does the Bible's salvation story give the entire Bible context?
- ➤ How does it unify the entire Bible?
- ➤ How does the Bible progressively reveal the salvation story as we read it to the end?
- ➤ Why must we understand the move from the old covenant to the new covenant to grasp the salvation story?

Questions concerning the assignment

1 Thessalonians 5:1–11:

- ➤ What did you observe from this passage?
- ➤ What questions came to mind as you studied?
- ➤ How does 1 Thessalonians 1–4 help us to understand the message of this passage?
- ➤ What Old Testament passages provide background for this passage?
- ➤ What did you learn about "the day of the Lord" in the Old Testament?
- ➤ How does that help you better understand this passage?
- ➤ How would you like to apply this passage?

Session #11

Questions concerning "Ponder the Application"

> ➢ Why is the application of a study so vital?
> ➢ Why is it so easy to ignore the application part of Bible study?
> ➢ How does 2 Timothy 3:16–17 help you learn how to apply a passage?
> ➢ Why is it essential that we keep the gospel in mind as we consider how to apply Scripture to our lives?
> ➢ How can the Holy Spirit help us with application?
> ➢ Why must we keep in mind the aim of the passage as we apply the Bible?

Questions concerning the assignment

1 Thessalonians 5:12–28:

> ➢ What did you observe from this passage?
> ➢ What questions came to mind as you studied?
> ➢ What did context, linking words, and structure tell you about this passage?
> ➢ Is the salvation story relevant to this passage? If so, how?
> ➢ What kind of message statement did you come up with for this passage?
> ➢ What application did you feel compelled to work on?

Session #12

Questions concerning "Review"

➤ Do you have any questions about the "Bible Pathway" diagram?

➤ Have you learned better how to observe and ask good questions of the text? How might you still improve in these areas?

➤ What have you learned about the importance of context?

➤ How does the structure and message flow influence how you think about a passage?

➤ Why is the Bible's salvation story key to understanding any passage of Scripture?

➤ What must we understand about the original readers before we can completely grasp what a passage is saying?

➤ How does a message statement help us understand the intent of a text?

➤ What have you learned about the importance of applying Scripture?

➤ What do you think Paul most wanted to communicate through 1 Thessalonians?

➤ What book of the Bible are you going to study next, and who might you invite to join you in that study?

About the Author

Al Lewis was a senior pastor with the Evangelical Free Church of America for twenty-three years before joining ReachGlobal and forming the Pastoral Training Team. He has developed the Pathways Bible Study method that is being used to train over 5,000 pastors and leaders worldwide in Bible study methods and preaching. He has now used that method in developing the *Pathways Bible Study Method* as a small group resource to teach laypeople how to do careful Bible study. Al and his wife, Edie, travel extensively and train pastors and wives in numerous countries. All proceeds from this book help fund this work.

Made in the USA
Monee, IL
02 September 2021